CILLA McQUEEN
FIRE-PENNY

CILLA McQUEEN

FIRE-PENNY

OTAGO

Published by University of Otago Press
PO Box 56/Level 1, 398 Cumberland Street
Dunedin, New Zealand
Fax: 64 3 479 8385. Email: university.press@stonebow.otago.ac.nz
First published 2005
Copyright © Cilla McQueen 2005
ISBN 1 877372 05 6
Cover illustration: *Dawn Chorus*, Cilla McQueen, 2004.
Illustration, p. 48: *Pounamu*, Cilla McQueen, 2004.
Back cover photograph by Alan Dove, courtesy IN Magazines.
Printed in Hong Kong through Condor Production Ltd
Published with the assistance of Creative New Zealand

ARTS COUNCIL OF NEW ZEALAND *TOI AOTEAROA*

POEMS

ST KILDA VOICES

WEATHER

A WIDOW'S SONGS

ST KILDA VOICES

RITE

A holy spring wells in a pool
fringed with blue iris
beside our church of iris thatch.

In the sun's good time,
we walk with our dead
to the graveyard, Cill Chriosed,

telling the bones beneath each knoll,
following the shadow of the mountain
as it draws across the Plain of Spells.

THE LAST GREAT AUK

When sternly the minister
expunged from our discourse
the ancient spells and poetry,
we became as gloomy
as if we had gazed on the ninth wave.

A great white bird – a portent
couched in deceptive beauty?

So fervent our self-examination
it caused us to despatch,
on the stac's altar,
the last Great Auk in Scotland,
for fear she be a witch.

LOCKS AND MIRRORS

Since we do not see ourselves
apart from the country
or each other, we have no use

for locks nor mirrors –
except the whittled wooden lock
for the door of our Sassenach prisoner;

except that still, reflective pool
in which the King of Norway's son
failed to see us creeping up to drown him.

THE CLEFT OF THE IRISHMAN

In the end, we allowed him up.
He was starving and scarcely a threat.

We had left him down there for a week,
in case he proved a supernatural occurrence.

Our suspicion is born of experience.
Nevertheless, he had a serviceable boat.

He came up. He came up drunk and thin
and raving, blown away from Ireland by a squall,

with no provisions but the keg of whisky
intended for his brother's Christmas party.

IN THE CLEFT OF THE BLANKETS

Roll them around us in a cocoon,
Our bodies on the hillside under the stars.

Nubbly tweed against my skin,
I cling as close to you as lichen.

Flesh falls away like the bark of wild fuschia.
The least willow is crippled by the wind.

The end of it all will be death,
sea-tongue, rock-tooth.

What will become of us, in time?
Bones, stars, brittle remnants.

FIRE-PENNY

Flint rakes
rosy quartz
fire-penny –
light leaps,

dry wisps
smoulder,
flare,
unveil your face –

thus in time
will I conjure
your image
in lamplight,

intangible
as lizard shadows
fleeting
among stones.

WEATHER

TO AN UNKNOWN POET

I was in the middle
of your poem on the internet
when the electricity went out.

You disappeared and left me
mid-sentence in the darkened room,
whereat I lost the gist

and wandered out to the kitchen to poke the fire.
I cannot tell whether you resolve
the unspoken thing,

or whether it will return to haunt us.
In the sudden darkness
I was leaning towards you

impossibly far, stroking
your temple and whispering
incomprehensible fragments –

WEATHER

If this is the end of the world then it's not too bad –
the wind is fierce but the house stands fast,
now and again a deep giggle running through it.
Fires burn brilliant in the huddled cottages

from which smoke pours and eddies in the gusts.
The sky turns dark and light as if great hands
passed mysteriously over the sun.
People slump by the fireside grumbling at the newspaper

secretly glad to be staying at home eating pikelets.
At this end of the world there is plenty of weather.
We do what we must when it needs to be done,
in our own time, which is of an elastic nature.

TRYSTING

In the rove of birds
a butterfly wing
fans an eyelash breeze
to stir the garden

where insects hover,
seeds crack with joy
take root and flower
in the light of love.

Undersea currents
fanned by fish
carry their younglings
to hatcheries deep

in submarine mountains
above whose peaks
the shimmering sky meets air
in the rove of birds

where hearts open kindly
as earth to seed,
tree to wind
soul to soul, trysting.

MUSE

White bib,
a black spot on her nose,
she dims.

Fur clumped,
yin-yang markings smudged
by a burnt patch from the heater
whose radiance she contemplates
immobile as a nun.

Pray for the grace of electricity, Lucille,
lest memory fail
of you who survived
a house on fire and two Staffordshires.

Who walked with dignity,
not inciting chaos.

Whose purr is soft and loud.
Whose sheathèd paw, with kind concern,
touches my cheek as I might touch
a flower petal, waking.

Lest you flicker and die –
three hardy strays observe our door.

THE FAIRIES RATTLE THEIR SPOONS

I heard on the radio
a scientist wants to make a crack
reaching to the centre of the earth.

Under the star-studded night-blue
ceiling of the cinema
Douglas Bader had no legs.

The desert blossomed with amazing speed.
One by one the little lights went out.
The sky grew tatty.

He declares he can do it with molten iron,
using gravity to force an arrow into her heart.
The purblind trust the usherette.

Your icecream might fall off.
You journey to the centre of the earth,
scared but determined.

Rather than the scientist staking her
like a vampire or a witch, to plumb her soul –
she might just close her legs and choke him.

STOAT'S SONG

Flick of a sinuous body
in lounge suit. Teeth.
I find you deliciously musical,
O eggs, thrill
to throttle shrill cadences,
plumb your skinny holes!

Ah piteous nest
of silken flesh exposed
to my spry jaw,
soothe me and sing to me within!
Innocence drowns in my throat.
All the trees are empty.

Scarce leisure to preen the brows
of supple stoats, sated with song.

POSSUM

Possum play possum in order to deceive opponent. Opossum [from Algonquin *aposoum*]. Possum. I am able. Stir the possum [Aust. slang]: to cause trouble. Phalanger. Arboreal marsupial. Phalange/phalanx/phalanger, bones of fingers and toes/ flying phalanger/ spiderweb/ webbed hind toes/ long spears behind a wall of overlapping shields/ closely ranked unit/ marsupial/ external pouch. Arboreal: of or resembling a tree; living in or among trees. Arbor: tree, rotating shaft in a machine on which a milling cutter or grinding wheel is fitted. Grinding down the bush. A myriad milling operations. Fixed. Axle: a bar or shaft on which a wheel revolves [C17: from ON *öxull*]. Axletree. Axe. Waste the bush faster than axes. Axis: A real or imaginary line about which a body can rotate or about which an object, form, composition or geometrical construction is symmetrical. One of two or three reference lines used in coordinate geometry to locate a point on a plane or in space. The second cervical vertebra. Stem and root of a plant. Alliance between states to coordinate foreign policy. Line of symmetry of an optical system, optics. Line passing through the centre of a lens. [C14: from L: axletree, earth's axis; rel to GK axon, axis.] Arbor or axle, spin or hold still about axis. Phalanger, Australian arboreal marsupial having dense fur and a long tail. Also flying phalanger. [C18:via NL from GK *phalaggion* spider's web, webbed hind toes.] Phalanx: ancient GK and Macedonian battle formation of hoplites presenting long spears from behind a wall of overlapping shields. Any closely ranked unit or mass of people. A number of people united for a common purpose. Any of the bones of the fingers and toes. A bundle of stamens.

Possum,
therefore I eat.
My ruthless arboreal phalanx
mills by teeth.

A WALK UPSTREAM

Trout and White are walking up a stream. Sounds of rubber boots, stones, water.

White You could say it trembles.
Trout With anticipation?
White On the brink. Eggshell.
Trout Of hope? Falling?
White Grace? Hovering.
Trout A dragonfly.
White Exactly.

Trout I debate the advantages of the one over the other, so that when I leap –
White Look out – too bad. Here, give me your hand.
Trout Thanks. Up to the knee.
White Occupational hazard.

Crackling branches, sounds of effort.

White Who's this on the bank?
Trout Neck! Well met!
Neck Trout of Fish and Game, old boy. Good condition!
Trout White, Egg Board.
White Pleased to meet you.
Trout Neck, of the racing fraternity.
Neck Checking the watercourse?
Trout Ensuring an even flow.
Neck Mind if I join you?

Neck climbs down the bank. They continue upstream, occasionally jumping stones and wading through small rapids.

Trout Until I was joined by my friend White, who has distracted me with semantics.
White Head of a pin. At a molecular –

Neck	Now you see it, now you don't?
White	In terms of the benzene molecule for instance –
Trout	There! Over there!

They stop. Water flowing over stones, into pools. Birdsong.

Neck	Ripples? Under the water?
White	Quivering. It trembles.
Neck	Whitebait?
Trout	Give me lampreys. A surfeit. In butter.
Neck	You might find one under these banks.
Trout	Turning to bite its tail in the frying pan. Delicious.
Neck	A coiling, a succulent morsel, head to tail in a golden ring.
White	Exactly. Molecular, neither here nor there.
Neck	A delicacy.
White	Ouroboros.
Trout	Certainly. A taste that trembles on the brink of roundness.

They continue, with effort.

Neck	Heard of the Crusader, Trout?
White	Ford?
Neck	Rabbit, my friend. Very good for stir-fry. Breed them in Oz.
White	Are we going much further?
Trout	Public release at Oreti Beach 1863. Speeches and songs, toasts to the ardent new citizens of our verdant land, gambolling off into the sandhills.
White	Gathered here together on the occasion of the unconditional release of the binary tree –
Neck	Procreation, eh, Fish and Game? No telling how far it'll go.
Trout	Nature only needs one pair of bunnies.

Fade out sounds of them going on. Somebody slips, is rescued, they continue. Birdsong and the sounds of water take over.

NEWBORN

Softly as opening wild iris
her long fingers touch the air

on the first of Spring. She lifts
a silver eyebrow, admitting

a garden, a red spade, a tree
with a sparrow in it. Curiously

as Alice is in the world,
the world is in Alice.

THE COMPANY OF POETS

I was standing at the Rattray St bus stop
when along came James K Baxter.
I hope, he said, in heaven,
to come among the company of poets,
Dylan Thomas, for instance,
we'd have a lot in common.

On the bus I told him that my grandfather had died.
Popped the bubbleskin, out of this world,
skin between this one and the other,
greater, world beyond world,
Amen, he said.

It is not much.

Another time I was peeling onions
when there was a knock at the door
and in came James K Baxter,
collecting for the Salvation Army.
I opened my purse and showed him my last dollar.
That's exactly how much I need, he said,
and popped it in his collection box.

GLIMPSE

I dreamed dawn light on stone
arched over flagstone and birds in rafters;
a courtyard where my friend unloaded
bedding from a truck, explaining as he passed
that there were thousands still to come
and he was making houses ready.

I thought of mansions, knowing him dead,
that it might be the edge of heaven where we stood,
but it was more familiar than I imagined heaven –
a grassy clearing in the bush, a sounding river.
We bystanders, behind some sort of skin
or one-way mirror, touched not nor took part –

it left no terror in my heart, for I had gone
to death and seen the people.

EDGEWAYS

Your voice curls out like smoke on a still day;
you will not let me get a mild enquiry in
edgeways, such as, Where are we going?

This I blurt; it lazes back laconically,
Wherever you like, and goes on mesmerising,
but it is not the answer I need.

Coming up London Street past the Globe,
a stretch traced all over with invisible ink –
the LP of 'Revolver' for instance, spinning down the hill,
cast from the hand of a tall dark man,

the same of whose brave kayak
once in the flooded Leith
remained but a broken paddle, at the mouth –

peripherally, your face a Giacometti
disappearing at the edge of reflection
into a thin line, no matter to speak of.

I remark the lyric way you writhe, your scales
in smoothly curving surfaces and coils, lazily
as your pale hand wafting me
right, up Stuart Street in a haze
of Central Otago Pinot Noir;

we might be anywhere, mist clearing in peaks
above the dash as we head over the top and down into the valley,
Where now? producing a cynical jeer;
nothing precisely.

Hand-jive, driving round the old circuit,
up Stone, down High, hoping for an answer
in time for decisions, perhaps the opportunity

to steer around to the pi-minus cloud
of benzene's molecular ring
and its resonant, parlous symmetry,

in illustration of whose behaviour
Kekulé divined, while dozing by the fire
dreaming of atoms dancing,
the self-devouring ouroboros, elegant
representation of benzene's veritable aura;

this snake, by serendipity, the symbol
of the antique ring which was all that remained
of the Flammable Lady,
in whose disturbing case of spontaneous combustion
fifteen years before,
his evidence had been forensic.

Still no real answer.
There was however, also a rumour
she had drunk so much alcohol that she ignited.

(for John Dickson)

ANTIPHONY
(letter to Peter)

If you could see this jet
fire-seeded sky,
chill here with me
on a plastic chair
on the verandah, we'd hear Bluff hum
while lines of sodium and magnesium
bridge and wharf lights
bleed to black,
inexactly
as on other nights, other verandahs,
another port – a kauri pew,
wings on the sill of an inside-out
lit window,
scrying the dark
insistent stars, fireflies –
we have talked of poetry.
You will know by now that the white ants you mentioned
have reached the far south.
Queenstown and her surrounding vineyards
house an active nest. The ants head south
in convoy, to eat a chunk of coast.
They thread their way to Bluff,
buy an icecream, take a photo of the signpost,
turn around and go back north,
having been there, or here,
as the case may be, as the mood
returns me
to that wineshop, Peter,
long ago
where we drank Bakano, talked and danced
until the floor began to singe.

P.S. the path the ants trace is a figure eight,
around the south and north and crossing at Cook Strait.

CAKE

The snapdragons remind me of the American
who came up to me once in a coffee bar
exclaiming loudly, 'You eat like a snake!'
I put down my cake. 'I beg your pardon?'
'A snake. And you're so small!'

It was true. The slice was very tall,
I had to open wide to get it in.
Unhinge my jaws. Cream on my chin,
I had been oblivious of my surroundings,
invisible, on a foreign planet.

AN IMP

Not the tin shed in the empty section
nor the immediate white cat with the patch

on its side like a hole,
but the imp in my eye his eye spat.

Imagination closed on it
quick as a fist, a black spar.

It queers my inner sight.
It cannot be dissolved by time.

LIFEBOAT

'A winning reputation as a tourist destination.'
'The greenest lifeboat in the world.'
Close the shoreline? Doc defend us!
Chop their arms off when they try
to climb aboard, lest all alike be lost?

Wakatipu wake with sewage in his mouth,
Queenstown slide off his lap into the lake,
the monorail buckle under the weight of visitors,
King Kong swallow his delectable actress,
the banks collapse, the river flood, some war begin?

MAILBOAT

No more will the bumblebee postie
wobble up to my letterbox with news from Skye,
Fraser Anderson.

In a St Kilda mailboat
I'll seal my last words to you,
and a penny for the stamp,
in a little wooden boat
buoyed by a sheep's bladder,
with a red flag on the mast;

'Please Open' burned
with a red-hot poker on the deck,
and post it in the ocean.

Was it putting out the neighbour's rubbish tin
That felled you, or Drambuie?
Slainte! For you, a toast to the Prince.

SHADE

Now the body of Wombat feeds the garden,
his juices enriching the rose.

What would I not give to touch again
his scarred black leather nose

the amber hair grown back,
not quite closed over,

to pat his warm shoulder
beside me – he'd open one eye

and grunt as he used to
grunt contentedly.

EVOCATIONS

Marian reads in a bare kitchen
at a table piled with books,
light on her forehead, her fair hair.
She looks at me and laughs aloud,
bright-eyed.

Marilyn reads in an armchair,
lamplight on her hair, the open book,
firelight on the cosy clutter of the room.
She turns the page.
She lifts her head and speaks a line of poetry.

Marilynn on the verandah draws the light
on mountains reflected in water,
smooths colour with her fingers.
Cosmos is purring quietly
among orange begonias.

When I call them
my friends appear without hesitation,
complete with surroundings,
handwriting, tone of voice, cast of thought,
familiar timbre of their laughter.

They appear as a radiance in my nerves.

JOANNA

Her hands lay colour light
as lips on paper

with the utmost care,
in faith the soul may leave us

as the sun the hills,
effacing shadows with all shadow,

or the moon the sea, reflection
rippling into time between,

the space in the world that held her
invisibly healing.

(for Pascal)

A BLUFF PANTOUM

Let the wind blow east, let the wind blow west,
The waves crash on the rocky shore;
My Jim is the man I love the best,
He keeps our anchorage secure.

The waves crash on the rocky shore –
He's wise in knowledge of the sea;
He keeps our anchorage secure,
For I love him and he loves me.

He's wise in knowledge of the sea,
And the swift mysterious ways of fish;
For I love him and he loves me –
He's my sweetest herb, my tastiest dish.

And the swift mysterious ways of fish
Are as deep and calm as our happiness;
He's my sweetest herb, my tastiest dish
In our favourite spot in Paradise.

As deep and calm as our happiness,
My Jim is the man I love the best;
In our favourite spot in Paradise,
Let the wind blow east, let the wind blow west.

(for Robyn)

SUNDAY

Chainsaw across the road – too late –
goodbye cabbage tree.
It blocked their view untidily.
They hate dead leaves getting twisted up in the mower
when they groom their green front.

Wind scours the valley, washing strangles on the line,
fishing nets, crayfish pots, salt scent –
'Thou gavest me the first honied fulmar' –
titi on the kitchen bench, fresh island bounty.

Wind swinging southerly – in for a pasting –
storm sweeps in with a horsehair brush.

Gales of laughter rock the kitchen –
the dog who ate eleven crayfish tails,
the dog who ate all the pauas,
the dog who could spell,
the dog who got washed off the fishing boat
and came in again paddling like hell on the next wave.

The dog who understands your every move,
whose strength is beyond your own.

Beneath the sea, the oysters
rock gently in their beds,
while armoured crayfish troop around the coast.

SHEEP ENCOUNTER

I looked up and saw a sheep
by the compost heap.
She stood impassive, as if carved in soap.

She was staring at the garden
ruminatively,
with some disdain.

I caught her eye.
She stopped chewing,
and fixed on me her solemn gaze.

A good ten minutes
she meditated thus,
on my occurrence in her field of vision.

And I on hers. It seemed to be
a sort of heaven.
Then, without a flicker of expression,

she turned her woolly bottom round
and went back through the hedge to Charlie's.

MUSEUM ATTRACTIONS, GORE

The flipside of the Gold Guitar
is perhaps the ancient African figures.

Tough glass encloses
the furious power in their wood bodies.

You may wander in the labyrinth
and stare at them without reprisal –

they have been tranquillised –
examine them until they are not strange,

in the manner of the bald soldier
whose torch probed the mouth of the captured

dictator; ponder your own psyche
through the glass that blocks the tapu.

A DOOR

Grainy sapways in the panels,
a fingerplate as smooth as piano keys;

a keyhole-cover
like a black pawn, tilted

over a brass-edged keyhole;
the door opening inwards.

Once I dreamed a zealous
surgeon had inserted

a round brown doorknob
in the middle of my back.

It seemed I was to be
some sort of interface.

Dream-language jells peculiar
when it hits the light.

A WIDOW'S SONGS

OVER THE BACK

Haloed with spray
in a southerly gale,
a rocky and treeless
descent to the strait

where the roaring ocean
swipes the rocks
and I am a wisp of fleece
on a barbed-wire fence

since he is gone,
passed on, like a storm,
cut a track
over the back

STARLINGS

'Bats in the belfry!' your legs
disappearing through the manhole,
'Come to me, birdies!'

Under the eaves, the starling chicks
are growing louder.
I cannot see me going up like you.

I cannot see me holding the ladder
as you come down
with a squawking bag,

jump the last rungs
and kiss me, grinning,
without tears.

BREAD

Frosty morning, ash
in a golden cloud
above the ashcan.

With fresh-splintered kindling and
full coal bucket stagger in
like a drunken sailor, a cheerful

blaze, push in the damper
so flame streaks over
and Orion hums –

I think of you
riddling the fire,
enjoying my bread
and cannot make it

FLAX

At the reservoir flax flames
in curving pods
on strong dark stems like oiled hair.

You make a boat of stems
with a green blade sail
and send it chiselling through clouds
in peat-bronze water.

Fixed, indelible,
mordant resin in the heart.

THE LANGUAGE OF BLUFF

The language of Bluff
is tender and blunt
when it comes to love.

Your fingers to my temple,
a soft, rough touch.

With your fisherman's knife
you slash a red bloom
from the rosebush, Erotica.

You read me cloud-currents,
tweak my ears to the westerly
rumbling storm-breakers
out beyond Auahi.

Your afterimage
inscribes the present;
your absence
a sort of sickening enchantment.

THIRD MOON

Kelp coils and recoils endlessly.
Ocean strokes granite with a sure, harsh pulse.

The rip is cracking at the harbour heads,
huia feathers of an ancient house.

I won't find you hanging around these rocks
and paths all night, gazing at heaven.

I think you've gone to Ganymede,
to be cup-bearer to the gods.

FROST

Time comes when my compass
trembles to your true absence

and I must turn you
to the third person,

whispering to the kowhai,
the patient constructions of spiders,

to the frost, he is history, gone
from this round world, he is starlight.

ACKNOWLEDGEMENTS

Some of these poems have been published in the literary magazines *Landfall, Rattapallax/Fusebox* e-zine, *Poetry International, Glottis* and *Fulcrum*. 'Evocations' was written for the anthology *It Looks Better On You* (Longacre Press, 2003).

This collection was written with the help of a grant from Creative New Zealand.

Acknowledgements are due to Mary Harman for information from her book *An Isle called Hirte* (MacLean Press, 1997).

Some of 'A Widow's Songs' have been set to music by Anthony Ritchie.

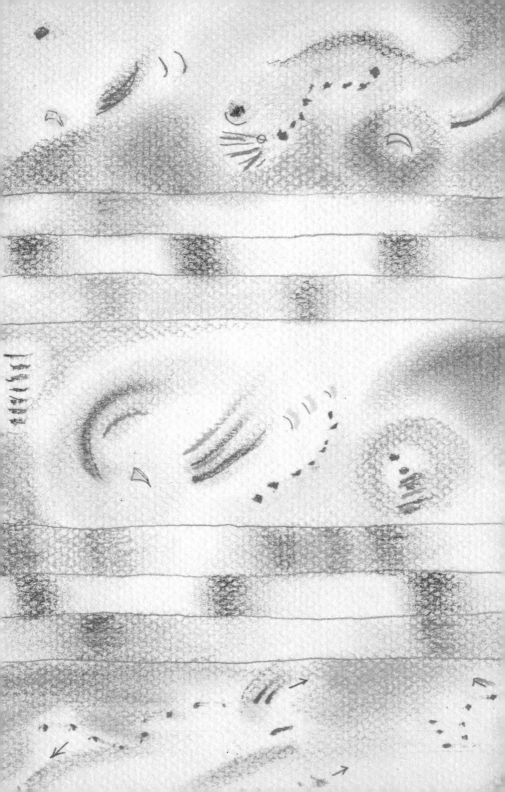